RAIN. SOME FISH. NO ELEPHANTS.

Y York

BROADWAY PLAY PUBLISHING INC
224 E 62nd St, NY, NY 10065
www.broadwayplaypub.com
info@broadwayplaypub.com

Cover art by Ampersand Studio

I S B N: 978-0-88145-075-0
First printing: December 1989
This printing: November 2016

Book design: Marie Donovan
Page make-up: Adobe InDesign
Typeface: Palatino

RAIN. SOME FISH. NO ELEPHANTS. was originally workshopped at New Dramatists, Jean Passanante, Director of Literary Programs; Primary Stages, Casey Childs, Artistic Director; The New Theater of Brooklyn, Debra Pope and Steve Stetler, Artistic Directors; New York Stage and Film, Max Mayer, Artistic Director (all directed by Mark Lutwak); and New City Theater, Pittsburgh, Marc Masterson, Artistic Director.

The world premiere was at Horizon Theater Company, Atlanta GA, Lisa and Jeff Adler, Artisitic Directors. The first performance was on 3 May 1989 with the following cast and creative contributors:

GENE	David Milford
ESTHER	Nita Hardy
JUNE	Suzanne Roush
EMILY	Joan Croker
JULIA	Nicole Torre
BLACKIE	Tony Vaughn
Co-directors	Jeff & Lisa Adler
Set designer	Dex Edwards
Costume designer	Yvonne Lee
Lighting designer	Kevin McDermott
Stage manager	Stephen Clifford

The New York premiere was at the New Theater of Brooklyn in April 1990. The cast and creative contributors were:

GENE .... Tim Halligan
ESTHER .... Angela Pietropinto
JUNE .... Julia Glander
EMILY .... Alice Haining
JULIA ....Arabella Field
BLACKIE/MORRIS ....Leon Addison Brown

Director .... Mark Lutwak
Assistant director .... Mark Lerman
Set ....Russell Parkman
Costumes .... Marianne Powell-Parker
Lights ....Howard Werner
Sound .... Tom Gould
Stage manager ....Lisa Ledwich
Music .... Philip Johnston
Music performance ....The Microscopic Septet

Acknowledgments: Certainly more actors performed in the workshops than I ever got to hire for productions. They were, as always, valuable beyond words.

CHARACTERS

GENE, *a white man in his late fifties*
ESTHER, *a white woman, forty-nine. His wife*
JUNE, *a white woman in her early twenties. Their daughter*
EMILY, *a white girl, twelve, she limps.* JUNE's *sister*
JULIA, *a white girl, twelve.* EMILY's *classmate*
BLACKIE, *a black man in his mid thirties.*

This one was always for Mom

(The curtain rises on an empty stage. The lighting on the cyclorama is blue. The location is the Chesapeake Bay. The stage is quiet for several seconds. Slowly, a sheep is lowered from the flies, then another, then another, until forty sheep are suspended in mid-sky. They represent clouds. A black man walks onto the stage carrying a torch. He sets fire to one, then another, then another of the sheep until all sheep are bleating and in flames. Just kidding. Turn page.)

ACT ONE

Scene One

(The interior of a house, a white living room, somewhere along the Chesapeake Bay, sometime in the future. Fishing gear hangs on a wall near the front door. The quiet sound of a steady rain. ESTHER *enters wearing rubber gloves; she maniacally dusts and cleans her way across the room. Enter* EMILY *from upstairs. She wears a strange prosthetic device on one foot.)*

EMILY: Looks great, Mom.

ESTHER: Great? Do you think it really looks great?

EMILY: Great's the only word for it.

ESTHER: What about...clean?

EMILY: Yeah, that's it. Great and clean.

ESTHER: Thank you, dear. Emily! Why are you wearing your false foot?!

EMILY: I'm going out.

ESTHER: It's your birthdate, you don't have to go out. If you don't have to go out, you don't have to wear your false foot.

EMILY: I told June I'd go with her to get ice cream.

ESTHER: It's your birthdate! June can go out by herself.

EMILY: She won't.

ESTHER: She will. She's brave. Go take that off.

(JUNE *enters from kitchen.*)

JUNE: You ready, Emily? Hi, Mom.

ESTHER: Emily is not going out on her birthdate. Your dad can go with you.

JUNE: He might not be back for hours.

EMILY: Why not? How long does it take to say "No thanks, buddy"?

JUNE: Dad is not going to say "No thanks, buddy."

EMILY: Is, too.

ESTHER: Come along, Emily. June, Emily and I are removing her false foot. She does not have to go out.

(EMILY *and* ESTHER *go upstairs.* JUNE *sighs, exits to kitchen.* GENE *comes in from outside. He is carrying a fish and fishing rod. He wears a rainslicker. He is wet.*)

GENE: Hey, everybody, come look at this. Esther!

ESTHER: *(Offstage)* In a minute, Gene.

(GENE *looks around, goes to the closet, finds a rainslicker. Puts it on the table, puts the fish on the slicker, starts to gut it.* JUNE *enters wearing rubber boots, looks into the closet.*)

JUNE: Why aren't you at the lab, Dad? I hope you were cooperative today. Where's my… What are you doing?

GENE: Don't yell. I hate it when you yell.

JUNE: That's my slicker!

GENE: How about this fish?

JUNE: Don't clean fish on my slicker.

GENE: It's a drum.

JUNE: Alright, it's a drum. Outside! You do that outside.

GENE: It's raining.

JUNE: Big news! It's been raining since '55. Why are you even here?!

(Enter ESTHER, *she dusts the steps.* JUNE *blocks the view of the fish from her.* ESTHER *goes to the kitchen.)*

ESTHER: Emily was wearing her false foot, today of all days. Gene, *you* can go with June to get ice cream. Nobody has to go outside on their birthdate. This banister looks very clean. And great. The cake is in the oven and *it's* going to be great. And clean, maybe. Better than anything you could purchase, I'll tell ya. Don't get too wet, June. Don't leave without saying goodbye. *(She disappears into the kitchen.)*

JUNE: Did you see that?

GENE: No. I carefully avoided that *that* that you're referring to.

JUNE: You know what she's doing, don't you? She didn't even look at us.

GENE: Help me clean this.

JUNE: Not that there's anything here to see.

GENE: I want to have it ready for the party.

JUNE: Birthdate parties aren't for fish. They're for ice cream, and soda. They're for sugar rush! It's dripping on the rug!

GENE: For your mom.

JUNE: You're just encouraging it.

GENE: It makes her happy. What else am I supposed to do?

JUNE: I don't know. Something. *(Pause)* What happened at the meeting? When are you going back? *(No answer)* Please don't play games with me. *(Sigh, resigned)* Where'd you get the drum?

GENE: Caught it.

JUNE: Dad! You didn't catch it. They're extinct. Did you steal it from the lab? If they send an Inspector—if you embarrassed me—

GENE: Out on the Chesapeake Bay, three foot seas, by myself. Knew it was a drum. You can always tell when it's a drum on the line. Extinct? You just gotta know where to catch 'em.

JUNE: Whose boat?

GENE: Mine.

JUNE: Dad—

GENE: It was really cold. Cold and…guess what?

JUNE: What?

GENE: Raining!

JUNE: You don't have a boat anymore.

GENE: Found the *Proud Esther* in the middle of the fleet, sitting there all sad and little and unused. I could have taken a destroyer. Nobody woulda noticed.

(JUNE *sighs.*)

GENE: Maybe I'll take a destroyer next time.

JUNE: *(Cleaning up the fish)* You're not going to take a destroyer.

GENE: Ever think you'd see a drum again? What are you doing?

JUNE: I'm cleaning this up before Mom sees it and gets ideas. You've lost your whole mind. *(She wraps up the fish in the slicker, exits to the kitchen.)*

GENE: *(Sings* Mule Skinner Blues*)* "Hee hee hee hee heeeeee! Ha ha ha ha ha ha!"

(Enter EMILY *without her false foot. She limps.)*

EMILY: Is this the entertainment for the party?

GENE: *(Sings)* "He he he he, heeeeeeeee! Ha Ha Ha ha ha ha!" Dance, Emily?

EMILY: That's a laugh.

ESTHER: *(Peeks in from the kitchen)* Gene, don't go picking on Emily. You can just leave her alone this one day of the year. What's that smell? *(She enters the living room.)* Hmm. Yes, I recognize it, but I can't identify it. Yes, it's a familiar, but as yet unidentified smell. *(She sniffs along the wall.)*

EMILY: Where you going, Mom?

ESTHER: Where am I going? I'm going to the kitchen. The kitchen is where I go, and I am going there now.

EMILY: Behind you. *(Guides her toward the kitchen)* This way, Mom.

(JUNE enters from kitchen carrying her bloody slicker.)

JUNE: They'll never issue me a new slicker. You all right, Mom?

ESTHER: Fine, fine. You can sing your tune, Gene, just don't pick on Emily. *(She exits to the kitchen, sniffing and dusting.)*

GENE: *(Sings)* "Hee hee hee hee heeeeeee."

JUNE: Is anybody going with me? *(Annoyed at the singing)* Dad!

GENE: *(Sings)* "Ha ha ha ha ha ha!"

EMILY: No. If Dad's going to lose his mind, I want to stay and watch it.

JUNE: Do you think anybody'll show up?

EMILY: No! Nobody ever has and nobody ever will.

JUNE: I thought your teacher made an announcement.

EMILY: Yeah. That was a big laugh.

GENE: As big as *(Talks)* "Ha ha ha ha ha ha"?

JUNE: Well, why am I going out there, if nobody's coming?

EMILY: *I* like ice cream.

JUNE: All right, I'll get ice cream. I'm taking your slicker.

EMILY: What's wrong with yours?

JUNE: See for yourself.

EMILY: Yuk.

GENE: It was a crucial element in the burial of my drumfish.

EMILY: A drum? Great.

GENE: Yep. Caught it today. On the high sea, hee hee hee hee hee hee.

EMILY: You didn't go on the high sea hee hee. Where'd you get it?

JUNE: I'm taking the eight-wheeler.

GENE: Wait a minute. Call your mom.

EMILY: You always forget.

JUNE: *(Sighs)* Mom! I'm going.

(ESTHER *enters wearing her rubber gloves.*)

ESTHER: Here I am. Goodbye, June. I love you.

JUNE: Goodbye, Mom. I love you. Goodbye Dad. I love you.

GENE: Goodbye, June. I love you.

EMILY: Goodbye, June, I love you!

JUNE: Oh, brother. Goodbye, all ready.

ESTHER: June, you know, you never know.

(JUNE *exits.*)

ESTHER: Emily, you don't have on your new dress. Is this a mistake?

EMILY: No.

ESTHER: But your new dress is for the birthdate party. It must be a mistake.

EMILY: Nobody's coming.

ESTHER: You should put on that new dress. Oh. Oh. Oh, my. What's this? What is this red? There is something red on the rug. It looks as if it's, yes, it is, it's wet. *(Happy)* There is a wet red spot on my white rug. Does anyone know what this might be? Well, I must know what it is before I can know how to deal with it. If it's wine, then I should put some very salty cold water on it, although I don't know where anyone in this house could find wine. If it's paint, why then I should get some paint remover. I hope it isn't blood. Why, if it were blood, it could be permanent. *(Sad)* I would have to look at this nasty red spot forever.

EMILY: It isn't blood. It's…Magic Marker. I was drawing a picture with Magic Markers and one of them leaked.

ESTHER: You were drawing! I'm so glad. You're such a talented girl. You draw; you make things. That's fine. I have to make the icing for the cake. Where are my gloves? Oh, right.

EMILY: Don't you want to fix the stain?

ESTHER: Of course, I want to fix the stain. I wouldn't leave a stain like that. I'll fix it later. *(Exits to kitchen)*

EMILY: But, Mom… *(Pause)* What happened at the meeting, Dad? What did they say after you told them where to stuff their petri dishes? June thinks you're going back. I told her it'd be a sunny-dry day before you ever worked in a lab again. Were they really mad?

I'll bet they were surprised. Nobody says no to them.
I'll bet they're shaking in their shoes.

GENE: Put this rod away for me.

EMILY: But, Dad, what did they—

GENE: Away. In the closet away.

EMILY: ...Okay. I haven't seen a drum in ages. Where'd
you get it?

GENE: I stole my boat back. Knew nobody'd be going
out.

EMILY: Nobody ever goes out.

GENE: Just me and the old boat. No fish either. Except
that drum. Tough fish. It pulled my boat around in a
circle.

EMILY: Where'd you catch it?

GENE: I'll show ya.

(GENE *pulls down a huge map of the Chesapeake Bay.
This is not the bay as we know it; it includes much of what
used to be the dry land of Washington, DC, Virginia, and
Maryland.)*

GENE: Here.

EMILY: By the monuments?

GENE: Yep. Tried the Smithsonian, but it was all
fished out. Had a feeling this guy'd be lurking in the
monuments.

EMILY: You could have capsized and drowned.

GENE: So what?

EMILY: For starters, it would have ruined my birthdate
for me for all time.

GENE: I was just trying to get you the perfect gift.
Remember this? *(He points to an area of land on the map.)*

EMILY: Arlington Burial Ground?

GENE: Gone.

EMILY: No!

GENE: Gone! Where's that crayon?

EMILY: I'll do it. *(She gets a blue crayon and colors the land area to match the water. Sad)* Wow.

GENE: I was kind of surprised myself.

EMILY: I *am* going to put on my new dress.

GENE: Your mom will like that.

EMILY: If she notices. *(Exits upstairs)*

GENE: Drowned? Capsized and drowned?! *(Singing)* "Ha Ha Ha Ha Ha Ha."

(ESTHER enters with a book and a squirt bottle.)

ESTHER: I can't find anything about magic marker stains. Now, if I knew what was in magic markers, I could look up the component parts. What's in magic markers, Gene?

(It's a gentler GENE, alone with ESTHER.)

GENE: Nobody knows what's in magic markers, Esther.

ESTHER: *(On hands and knees scrubbing)* This is a solution of water and vinegar.

GENE: That's for cat piss.

ESTHER: Now, Gene, nothing gets out cat piss. That's documented. Did you get Emily a present?

GENE: I did, but June stole it. I'll go see if I can find it. *(Exits to the kitchen)*

ESTHER: *(She scrubs the rug for a second, then shouts to GENE in the kitchen.)* Gene! Do you think I've become obsessed with stains because of this white carpet; or... do you think I got this carpet because I've become obsessed with stains?

GENE: *(Entering with fish)* Maybe.

ESTHER: *(Pause)* What's that?

GENE: Drumfish. Try fish oil for getting out the magic marker.

ESTHER: I've never heard of that.

GENE: Me neither. Might work.

ESTHER: Might. *(She takes a piece of the fish skin and rubs it into the rug.)* Hmm. I recognize this smell. It is a recent and familiar smell.

GENE: *(Hopeful)* Yeah, yeah?

ESTHER: Gene! This is a fish. I used to catch these. Big ones!

GENE: *(Hopeful)* Yes, you did. You were terrific, Esther.

ESTHER: *(A degree of lucidity previously unseen)* Hi.

GENE: *(Quietly)* Hi.

ESTHER: *(Looks around)* Looks like I've been busy.

GENE: Yeah.

ESTHER: Oh well. At least the place is clean.

GENE: Yeah.

ESTHER: Oh, Gene, I'm so worried…

GENE: Don't worry—I'll take care of you—

ESTHER: Not about me. June. She's becoming stuffy. A stuffy person. She doesn't sing anymore. Maybe you could remember another tune for us.

GENE: I could try again.

ESTHER: I remember when you first remembered the tune. You were tickling me. I went hee hee hee hee hee hee, and you sang "ha ha, ha ha ha ha." Too bad you can't remember the words.

GENE: Someday, maybe.

(ESTHER and GENE kiss.)

ESTHER: June used to sing it with you. She isn't sweet to Emily anymore. I think it's those people at the lab. Half-people. I don't like it. I'm going to talk with her. She should be doing good things. Then she would be happy. She could stop the rain. She could neutralize the acid. *(Drifting away, starting to clean)* She could play with her sister, or even go fishing with you. *(Gone away)* She could help me…dust. She could help me clean the carpet! Where's that fish skin?

GENE: Here it is.

ESTHER: *(Scrubbing)* Thank you, Gene. How does this look, Gene? Is it better?

GENE: *(Sad)* Fine. It's fine.

(The doorbell rings. ESTHER and GENE look at each other.)

ESTHER: The doorbell. June is out, but isn't June because she doesn't ring. Everybody else is here. That must be the party!

JULIA: Open up! It's raining!

GENE: A weather psychic.

ESTHER: Emily has a wide spectrum of friends.

GENE: No, she doesn't.

(Doorbell rings for a long time. GENE opens the door.)

GENE: *(To JULIA)* Stop that.

(Enter JULIA. She wears a fur coat, carries a satchel. A black arm is seen holding an umbrella over her.)

JULIA: Is this Emily's house?

GENE: It's my house.

(Pause, JULIA starts out.)

ESTHER: But Emily lives here.

JULIA: Is there a party?

GENE: What's it to you?

ESTHER: Yes, of course there's a party. It's Emily's birthdate and we're having a party. We're so glad you could come.

JULIA: My female elder made me. *(To the black arm)* Wait in the car. Keep the motor running, but don't asphyxiate yourself, Blackie.

(The arm disappears, the door closes.)

GENE: Blackie! This kid's got her own Blackie. La de da de da de da. And a Fakefur.

JULIA: This isn't a Fakefur. We don't have anything fake in our house. If it isn't real, my male elder won't buy it. We have real silver and real wood and real art.

GENE: I have a real pain in my behind.

(ESTHER pets JULIA's coat.)

JULIA: What are you doing?

ESTHER: The poor little things.

GENE: What do you do with all this really real stuff?

JULIA: We keep it in the vault, of course. Are you Emily's male elder?

GENE: Me? Noooooo. I'm her footman. And that's her lady-in-waiting.

JULIA: I'm Julia. I never get invited places. That's why Rena made me come. I wish she could see you both. I'd never have to leave the house again. *(She sits down, makes herself comfortable)* What are you doing with those big fish guts?

ESTHER: You see that stain? I was using those fish guts to get rid of that stain. But since the party's here, I'll put them away. *(She exits to the kitchen.)*

JULIA: Fishguts? Why doesn't she use Stainout?

GENE: She's a perfectionist.

JULIA: She's completely crackers. I didn't know people like her got past the eliminations.

GENE: Specimens of an earlier age. Like your Blackie.

JULIA: If it was up to me, anybody like that— Zap! Through the Space Disposal.

(Enter EMILY *in her new dress.)*

EMILY: What are you doing here?

JULIA: I was invited. Remember? Yuk. Unsettle my calm! Where is your false foot?!

EMILY: I don't have to wear it at home.

JULIA: Put it on!

EMILY: Not at home. I don't have to.

JULIA: I can't even look at you!

EMILY: Then why don't you leave!

JULIA: I can't leave. I brought you a present.

EMILY: *(Lying)* We...don't have presents at birthdates!

JULIA: Well, I can't take it back. Rena said I had to give it to you.

EMILY: Dad, uh, I mean, Gene, why don't you hang up her coat?

JULIA: Did you say Dad?

GENE: Of course not. She said "gad". "Eee gad, why don't you hang up her coat?"

EMILY: Well, why don't you?

GENE: It might bite me.

EMILY: I know. Poor little things. *(She pets the coat.)*

JULIA: Don't touch me! Put on your foot!

GENE: Emily, leave your foot where it is.

JULIA: This is awful! *(She takes a pill.)*

(A brief silence)

GENE: Do you want your coat hanged or not?

JULIA: *(Happy from her pill)* I'll wear it, thank you.

ESTHER: *(Offstage)* Gene, come help me fold this fish skin!

GENE: Excuse me, miss, I'm going to help your female elder with my drum. Don't worry, I'll be back. *(Exits)*

JULIA: Can I see it?

EMILY: See what?

JULIA: Your foot. I want to see your foot.

EMILY: Okay.

JULIA: Wow. Walk a bunch.

EMILY: No.

JULIA: I say so so you have to.

(EMILY sighs, walks.)

JULIA: That is so weird.

EMILY: It isn't weird, it's great. It's the one and only walk like this in the whole world.

JULIA: What's great about that? Do you really not give presents?

EMILY: Yes. We think it's barbaric.

JULIA: This whole domestic unit is a mess. Both female youngers are mutants and your elders are eliminatable.

EMILY: We are not mutants.

JULIA: Are, too. You got that weird foot and June works in a lab. Females don't work in labs. They only code female zygotes to eight.

EMILY: She's smart from being around Gene.

JULIA: It doesn't work like that! I told Rena nobody'd come to your party. Nobody likes you. You walk funny. You're a crippled freako strange thing.

EMILY: So what?! We are weird. You know what else? Gene has a boat. He caught a drumfish on it just today.

JULIA: No he didn't. Nobody has a boat. They fill up with rain and sink.

EMILY: I'll show you.

(EMILY *runs into the kitchen.* JULIA *runs over to snap secret pictures of the books.*)

JULIA: Wow, look at them all!

(EMILY *comes back in with the fish.*)

EMILY: What are you looking for?

JULIA: Nothing.

EMILY: You spy. You creepy snoop. Why don't you call your male elder and tell him we have books? I'll bet he's just dying to know.

JULIA: He knows you have books.

EMILY: You better tell him about *this* one. *Serious Stain Removal.* It's my...uh...Esther's favorite book. She reads it day and night. Sometimes she quotes from it. You better call him quick. I'm sure this is subversive. *(Pause)* Nobody likes you, either.

JULIA: Your female elder reads?

EMILY: So what?

JULIA: Unsettle my calm! *(Takes a pill. Smiles. Pause)* Is that a real dead fish?

EMILY: Yeah, fresh-caught today, you can tell by the blood. They don't sell them this messy, you got to catch it to get it to look like this. Gene is a hearty seaman, brave and true, with a boat. And this is a new dress. And we don't give presents because it's barbaric.

JULIA: How come you have a new dress if you don't give presents?

EMILY: It isn't a present. It's a coincidence. *(Pause)* Why don't you go home?

JULIA: I can't. Rena said I had to stay for the whole party.

EMILY: Why don't you wait in your eight-wheeler?

JULIA: We don't have an eight-wheeler. We have a stretch. With triple-thick protective glass. Rena told my Blackie to drive me home after the party. If he takes me home now, she'll yell at me.

EMILY: Esther never yells at me.

JULIA: Really? Never?

EMILY: Never.

JULIA: Not even when you get really dirty and bring mud in? You have a white carpet. I'd get killed if we had a white carpet.

EMILY: No. Esther likes dirt. It's her hobby.

JULIA: Come on.

EMILY: She talks to it and chases it around. She walks around all day looking for it and she's miserable until she finds it. Sometimes we have to bring it in special so she has something to do.

JULIA: Sounds like Stage Three to me.

EMILY: No, it isn't!

JULIA: Then Stage Four, then Zap, the Suicide!

EMILY: It isn't the suicide, it isn't. *(Lying)* She's always been like this.

JULIA: Oh, sure. What do you care, anyway? My female elder started, and I'm glad. *(Pause)* Are there going to be any games?

EMILY: I don't know. I didn't think anybody would come.

JULIA: Let's play Eliminator!

EMILY: No.

JULIA: I say so so we will.

EMILY: I don't know how.

JULIA: I'll show you. It's easy. It's fun. I have a kit.

(JULIA *goes to her satchel and takes out her Eliminator Kit. It contains a black sack, rope for tying hands, and a gag. She hands the sack to* EMILY.)

JULIA: Put this on.

EMILY: No. Let me be the Eliminator, and you put on the sack.

JULIA: Don't be ridiculous! I'd never be eliminated. Put this on. (*The gag*) Hurry up. I get to tie your hands. (*She does.*) And now, the sack. (*She pulls the sack over* EMILY.)

(JUNE *enters from outside with ice cream.*)

JUNE: There's a stretch outside, and it's got two Blackies... What's going on?!

JULIA: Oh, good, you can be the witness.

JUNE: Are you one of Emily's guests?

JULIA: I'm her only guest. I'm Julia. You gotta play.

JUNE: Is this a game?

JULIA: Of course, it's a game. It's Eliminator. (*Sonorous voice*) Emily! There has been a complaint against your walk. Your disgusting imbalance has unsettled citizen calm. You must be eliminated. (*To* JUNE) Go ahead.

JUNE: (*Upset*) What do I do?

JULIA: You say, "What is the identifying mark?"

JUNE: What is the identifying mark?

JULIA: Her stupid gimp walk. Walk, Emily!

(EMILY *does.*)

JULIA: Carry her to the Space Disposal.

JUNE: I don't think so.

JULIA: Come on, it's a game.

JUNE: Where is the Space Disposal?

JULIA: Anywhere. There. Put her on that chair. *(Big voice)* Take the sack off for the official identification. It's her, all right. Take off the gag. Now, Emily, jump into the Space Disposal.

(EMILY *jumps off the chair.*)

JULIA: Scream.

EMILY: No.

JULIA: You have to scream.

EMILY: It doesn't hurt.

JULIA: Yes, it does.

EMILY: The videos say it doesn't hurt.

JULIA: My male elder says they say that just so people don't make a fuss. I want you to scream.

EMILY: I'm not going to scream and that's that.

JULIA: You don't do anything right. *(To* JUNE) What are you doing?

JUNE: *(Untying* EMILY) This game is over.

JULIA: No!

EMILY: No more games. Gene! Esther!

(GENE *enters.*)

GENE: What's up?

EMILY: We need some entertainment.

GENE: What's that bag doing here?

JUNE: How about a story, Gene?

GENE: Story?! You ever been fishing, Julia?

JULIA: No.

(Enter ESTHER *with cake and lighted candles.)*

ESTHER: Sing with me everybody. *(Singing)* "Hee hee hee hee heeeee…"

JULIA: *(Horrified)* No singing!

ESTHER: Well, all right. Happy birthdate, dear Emily. Now make a wish and blow out the candles.

GENE: I wish for… *(Starts to blow out the candles.)*

ESTHER: Stop it. Now just stop it. It's Emily's wish.

*(*JULIA *blows out the candles.)*

GENE: But I have a great wish.

JUNE: Behave Gene.

GENE: Don't tell me to behave in front of creepy strangers.

JULIA: I don't mind.

EMILY: I'll bet you don't. Bet you can't wait to run home and complain to your male elder about us.

JULIA: I don't always complain.

EMILY: You complained about that little boy and they took him away in a sack.

JULIA: He was repulsive. He unsettled my calm. But I never complained about your false foot. I never said it unsettled my calm. I never had you taken away in the sack.

JUNE: What's your male elder do, Julia?

JULIA: He's an Inspector.

(A silence)

JULIA: I want some ice cream.

(ESTHER *and* JUNE *bustle.)*

ESTHER: June! Did you get ice cream!?

JUNE: Yes, yes. Right here it is.

GENE: Ice cream, ice cream, for the Inspector's female younger!

ESTHER: I'll get bowls! *(Exits to the kitchen)*

JULIA: Take the fish away.

GENE: Aw...

EMILY: No. It's my present. Leave the fish.

JULIA: A present? It's a present? There are presents!

EMILY: No. It is present. I want it present. It's messing up the rug nice. Esther'll have a ball, later. Right, Dad?

JULIA: Dad?

GENE: Bag. *(Points at it)*

JULIA: Let's play Eliminator some more. Let's eliminate...you. *(Points to* GENE*)*

GENE: I don't think so. Dancing!

JUNE: *(A warning)* Gene...

GENE: *(To* JULIA*)* Would you like to dance?

JULIA: Stop it. Dancing's not allowed.

(Enter ESTHER *with a large bowl.)*

ESTHER: Here is a large bowl. I think it's just perfect.

JULIA: Fill it up.

ESTHER: Yes, right to the very top. June, the ice cream.

*(*JUNE *plunks the gallon carton of ice cream into the bowl.* ESTHER *hands it to* JULIA*.)*

JULIA: Where's the spoon?

ESTHER: Spoon? Of course, you'll need a spoon. Oh, I forgot the spoon. *(She exits to the kitchen.)*

GENE: We never use spoons for ice cream. We usually eat it like this.

(GENE *opens the carton, gets a gob of brightly colored ice cream and pushes it in* JULIA'*s face.*)

JULIA: Eeeeeeeeeeeeeeee!

GENE: Open up the Space Disposal. Here comes a load of creeps! Mmmmmmmm, open it up, open it up. *(Pushes ice cream in her face)*

JULIA: Eeeeeeeeeeeeeee! You're crazy. You're all eliminatable. Eeeeeeee! There's ice cream on my coat. *(She exits.)*

GENE: My wish just came true. *(Sings victoriously)* "Hee hee hee heeeee heeeeeee."

(EMILY *and* GENE *join hands, do a little circle dance.* JUNE *gasps in disbelief and fear.* JULIA *re-enters with a black man in a three-piece suit. He is carrying a small suitcase.*)

JULIA: Here's your stupid present. You'll probably forget to feed it. *(She exits.)*

(Enter ESTHER *out of breath.)*

ESTHER: Spoon?!!

Scene Two

(Later that day. The living room. EMILY, GENE, *and* JUNE *are trying to tell a story to* BLACKIE—*who constantly tidies and does not sit. The map of the Chesapeake Bay is down.* GENE *refers to it now and again. The sound of steady rain.)*

GENE: We were drifting opposite the launching pad looking for bluefish. The girls were kids, but they could always handle a line. We see fish churning the water about half a mile away. I haven't seen fish break like that in years. In two seconds there's fish on every rod. I let the girls work the lines, Esther takes the helm, and I rig up my spinning rod and cast into the middle of the fish. Emily brings in a double header and her lines are crossing June's line and June's swearing up a streak. That one there has a mouth. Emily gets bit by one of the blues and starts to bleed and yell. June screams, "Not now!" and I'm standing on the bow jigging my line when suddenly I feel... something big. Now understand, I've got my spinning rod out there, and it's only got a twelve-pound-test line. And I got what feels like a hundred pounds of fish, so I'm a little more nervous than I would be if I was deep sea fishing and prepared. So I calmly say...

EMILY: About as calm as a hurricane.

GENE: I calmly say, "Cut the lines."

JUNE: I thought he'd seen a big shark and we were going to have to make a run for it.

GENE: The girls cut the lines, and Esther turns the boat toward the fish, and we let this baby run. He drags us out of the bay into the ocean before we even notice. About an hour's worth of this and I feel him get tired. So we start to reel him in.

JUNE: And then he jumps up in the air and he's longer than the boat.

EMILY: He was beautiful.

GENE: He knew he was beat. He just sort of gave up and let us reel him in.

BLACKIE: What happened to the fish?

JUNE: We let him go.

EMILY: You can't eat sailfish and they don't let you mount them anymore.

BLACKIE: Mount?

GENE: Mount. Preserve for posterity.

BLACKIE: Pardon me?

EMILY: Like museums with woolly mammoths and dioramas with cute scenes from life.

BLACKIE: Woolly whats?

JUNE: We've never seen them either. We just take his word for it.

BLACKIE: *(Confused/suspicious)* You went out on a boat today?

GENE: Yep. Caught me that drum.

BLACKIE: You went out on a boat they took away from you?

GENE: Correct.

BLACKIE: Without asking?

GENE: Correct.

BLACKIE: You could be eliminated for that.

EMILY: No, he couldn't. Not Gene.

BLACKIE: Everybody has to ask for permission.

EMILY: That's a laugh.

JUNE: Emily!

EMILY: Well, it is.

JUNE: Emily, it might not always make you happy, but the order of society can only be maintained if everyone follows the rules.

GENE: Thank you, June…the loon, scientific raccoon.

(Enter ESTHER with the cooked drumfish.)

ESTHER: I've cooked it. Look. It's beautiful. It's beautiful, Gene.

BLACKIE: Allow me, Miss. *(He takes the tray.)*

ESTHER: *(Sad)* Oh. Why are you holding my dish? Gene, why is he holding my dish?

GENE: He's helping.

EMILY: Don't you ever sit?

BLACKIE: No.

EMILY: Then I'm not going to sit either.

JUNE: Sit down.

EMILY: If everybody can't sit, then I'm not going to sit.

ESTHER: Me, neither! June.

JUNE: Oh brother. *(Stands, too)*

GENE: Me, neither. *(He lays flat on the floor.)* Blackie, drop food in my mouth would you?

BLACKIE: Certainly, sir.

EMILY: Unsettle my calm!

JUNE: *(To* BLACKIE*)* Don't encourage him.

EMILY: Please get up.

GENE: No.

EMILY: You gotta sit down, Blackie.

BLACKIE: Certainly, Miss.

(They all sit, GENE *gets off the floor.)*

GENE: *(Like a parrot)* Miss, Mister, Miss, Mister.

JUNE: Stop it, Gene. It's how they're trained.

ESTHER: What is your rating, Blackie?

GENE: Blackies aren't rated.

EMILY: How can you tell how smart they are?

GENE: What's the square root of six-thousand-five-hundred-twenty-four?

BLACKIE: …Eighty point…seven…seven…one…two…eight …two…

GENE: Like that.

EMILY: Wow.

JUNE: What were you trained for?

BLACKIE: Domestic maintenance, database management, and games.

GENE: You don't happen to know any tunes, do ya? *(Brief pause)* Tunes. *(Sings)* "Hee hee hee heeee heeeeeeee. Ha ha ha ha ha ha."

BLACKIE: No, no tunes. I know prepositions. About, above, across, after, against, along, among, around, at, before, behind, below, beside, between, beyond...

EMILY: How about history?

BLACKIE: No, of course not.

GENE: When are we gonna eat?

ESTHER: Well. Now. I mean it's here. We can eat it. I'll get the plates, and I'll get the forks, and I'll get the knives and the spoons.

GENE: Let Emily do it. I like to watch her walk.

EMILY: Oh, brother.

GENE: The only walk of its kind in the universe.

BLACKIE: Allow me, Miss. *(Exits to kitchen)*

ESTHER: *(Sad)* Oh. I want to get to get the plates and forks and knives and spoons.

JUNE: It's all right, Mom. He's just helping.

ESTHER: Gene, are the girls going to have to call us "Gene" and "Esther" forever?

GENE: I hope not. *(Goes to BLACKIE's suitcase, opens it, examines the contents)* Let's see what we got here. Change of clothes...camera *(Sarcastic)* wonder what that's for. And look here, June. *(He holds up a huge bottle of pills.)*

EMILY: Let me see them! "Life sustaining chemicals, Blackies only, one every hour, or as needed." Wow. What's wrong with him?

GENE: Nothing. They're just stoppers. What do you think, June?

JUNE: I don't think we'll have any problems with him, if that's what you mean.

GENE: Well, that won't be any fun. *(Dumps the pills into a waste basket)*

JUNE: You can't do that.

GENE: Go get me a messa C caplets.

JUNE: No.

GENE: You are getting stuffy.

JUNE: Oh, brother. *(Exits to upstairs)* I'm not going to be responsible for this.

EMILY: Why does he take a stopper every hour?

GENE: They never rated blackies. They don't need to dumb them down genetically if they're taking these.

EMILY: What's his potential, then?

GENE: Higher than yours.

(JUNE enters.)

JUNE: Here.

(JUNE hands GENE a bottle of similar pills. GENE fills BLACKIE's bottle with the new pills.)

EMILY: What are C caps gonna do for him?

GENE: Same as they'd do for you.

ESTHER: That'll be healthy gums, and healthy gums retain their teeth.

GENE: How's that look?

JUNE: They'd fool me.

GENE: *(Sarcastic)* Then I guess they'll fool anybody.

(JUNE puts the new pills back in the suitcase, returns the suitcase to where it was.)

EMILY: Why do they keep them at ten percent?

GENE: So they don't ask questions.

EMILY: What questions would they ask?

GENE: Somebody give her a stopper.

(Enter BLACKIE with plates, cutlery, etc. ESTHER trips him, he falls, there is a fuss.)

ESTHER: *(Happily)* What a mess! *(She starts to clean the mess.)*

JUNE: Are you all right? *(To ESTHER)* Why did you go and do that?

ESTHER: I needed a mess. Right now.

BLACKIE: I'll take care of it, Miss. Please don't be upset.

ESTHER: Upset about what?

BLACKIE: It's just broken dishes. The carpet isn't impaired.

ESTHER: Of course it is. Give me that! Don't you touch that. I'll clean it up.

BLACKIE: You might cut yourself, please…

ESTHER: What's it to you?

EMILY: *(Picks up the fish and drops it into the mess)* Here you go.

ESTHER: Oh, thank you, sweetie.

(ESTHER happily takes some debris to the kitchen. BLACKIE is upset by the events.)

ESTHER: I'll go get my book. *(Exits)*

JUNE: I wanted to eat that fish.

EMILY: Gene can catch another one.

JUNE: No, he can't. He was lucky to catch that one. You just carpeted the sole survivor. The species is extinct.

ESTHER: *(Enters, reading)* I'm sure it's in the index. Fish stains, fish stains. Somewhere.

GENE: I think you use magic marker.

ESTHER: Don't be silly. *(She starts to clean carpet while she reads.)*

EMILY: Are they really extinct?

GENE: It's the grim reaper-cussions of progress, right Blackie?

BLACKIE: Of course, Sir.

GENE: My name is Horace.

BLACKIE: I thought your name was Gene.

GENE: My name's Horace.

ESTHER: But nobody calls you that. How's this look?

GENE: A lot better. But it needs work, needs work.

ESTHER: Oh, good. I'll get some fluids. *(Exits to kitchen with book)*

JUNE: Gene used to be a gene mucker.

EMILY: *(To herself)* Last year there were zillions.

BLACKIE: Eugenics?

GENE: Correct.

BLACKIE: Unrated?

GENE: Unrated uncoded.

BLACKIE: I didn't know there were any left.

GENE: Just one. A minor miracle, wouldn't you say?

EMILY: Ohhhh!

(EMILY throws herself into GENE's arms, sad.)

GENE: Now, now. What's this? Affection?

EMILY: No more drumfish! *(She runs upstairs.)*

(Enter ESTHER reading from book.)

ESTHER: June, I need a lemon. *(Reads)* "To remove the odor of fish apply fresh lemon." I need a lemon.

JUNE: I'll get you one.

ESTHER: Today? Now? From the lab?

JUNE: Please don't ask me to go to the lab on my day off.

ESTHER: But I need a lemon, now.

BLACKIE: Pardon, Madam. Vinegar will work. Use it full strength.

ESTHER: It says lemon!

BLACKIE: I understand. But vinegar will work. Can I get it for you?

GENE: It's in the basement. I used it. Esther, why don't you take Blackie down to the basement? Show him around.

ESTHER: The basement? How did it get there? *(Taking off her shoes)* Blackie, would you like to see the basement?

BLACKIE: Yes, Miss. *(Takes off his shoes, rolls up pants.)*

ESTHER: I could have sworn it was under the sink. Now I left it under the sink. If it's not there, it's because somebody else moved it away. I would have replaced it, myself.

(BLACKIE and ESTHER exit.)

JUNE: What were you doing with vinegar?

GENE: The vinegar's under the sink. I just wanted a minute to think.

JUNE: *(Sarcastic)* Oh, you're going to think?

GENE: Don't be a wise guy. "The order of society can only be" what did you say, "maintained"?

JUNE: I don't know what I said! I'm just trying…and you're no help, and Emily—what can we expect from this guy? You know their genetic code as well as anybody.

GENE: Nope. Nobody knows their genetic code. They're chemically controlled. Let's wait until the stoppers wear off. Let this guy have an uninterrupted thought or two. See what happens.

JUNE: See what happens? He's a spy. You think he's a spy, don't you?

GENE: No, I think he's a professional photographer. We could ask him. He won't lie. Blackies can't lie.

JUNE: But then he'd also have to tell them that we asked him… Why did they send a spy? Dad! What did they say at the meeting? You told them you'd work again. You did tell them that, didn't you? *(No answer)* You are making me crazy, I am actually going to lose my mind.

GENE: You could always leave.

JUNE: And go where?

GENE: *(Sarcastic)* Accept a proposal of domestic sharing. Settle down with a nine or, even a ten.

JUNE: There is no more domestic sharing.

GENE: Aw.

JUNE: And there won't be until you code some zygotes!

GENE: Aw!

JUNE: After you go back to the lab, they'll come and take the Blackie away; we go back to the way it used to be.

GENE: *(Sarcastic)* The way it used to be? That good?

JUNE: You know, Dad, you wouldn't have to actually code a human zygote. You could tell them that you had to start slow. You had to experiment. Start with frogs. You could code frogs. You could do it for years.

GENE: Hmm.

JUNE: They'll take back the Blackie. They'll get off our back.

GENE: Why don't you code frogs?

JUNE: You're the only one who can.

GENE: *(Happily)* I know.

JUNE: But you could show me...

GENE: You're just dying to impress all them male lab techs.

JUNE: I am not! I just want to keep this family on the planet for as long as possible. Which is more than I can say for other members of this family.

(EMILY *enters carrying four cardboard elephants on sticks— one red, one white, one blue, and one black. The elephants wear decorative clothing. They have been made by* EMILY, *who has never seen an elephant.)*

JUNE: Oh, brother.

EMILY: It's for the drumfish, and we're gonna do it.

JUNE: Totally eliminatable.

EMILY: Well why don't you just call your buddies from work and have them sack me. Nobody's stopping you.

JUNE: It's just an expression, Emily. Don't be so sensitive.

GENE: That's right, Emily. When your sister tells you you're ready for the Space Disposal, you should take it in your crippled little stride. Give me the red one.

EMILY: No. You don't get one.

GENE: What's this?

EMILY: Blackie gets one.

GENE: I shall perform without costume. *(Begins to trumpet)*

(ESTHER and BLACKIE enter with vinegar.)

BLACKIE: I don't know this game.

GENE: You will.

ESTHER: Gene, it was under the sink the whole time. *(Holds up the bottle)*

GENE: Whadaya know?

EMILY: Here. *(She hands BLACKIE the black elephant.)* These are elephants, Blackie. Elephants are the only animals that helped with their own extinction.

BLACKIE: Just a moment please. *(He gets his pill bottle from his suitcase, takes one, pockets the bottle)* Elephants?

GENE: Great and noble beasts. Grew to a hundred feet high, weighed over fifty thousand tons. They ate trees.

BLACKIE: Trees?

EMILY: A long time ago, a zillion guys got together and tamed one wild elephant. Then that elephant helped tame other elephants. Pretty soon there wasn't a wild elephant left.

BLACKIE: And they died because they were tamed?

EMILY: No. The guys who tamed them used the elephants to pull up all of the trees to make a parking lot. When all of the trees were gone, the elephants died of starvation.

ESTHER: *(Scrubbing the fish stains with vinegar)* And they liked to dress up. That's why Emily has them in nice clothing.

EMILY: Naturally, they didn't dress for the forest.

BLACKIE: Did you make the replicas, Miss?

EMILY: *(Proudly)* Yeah. Gonna turn me in on an art violation?

BLACKIE: Is that a nose?

EMILY: Yes. They kept their treasures in it and lifted things. They could rip out trees by the roots.

BLACKIE: *(Visibly upset)* What are you going to do with the elephant replicas?

JUNE: Taming game.

ESTHER: Emily makes us do this game for every new extinction. Last week we did it three times.

GENE: How're you doing, Esther?

ESTHER: Fine, Gene. I wish I had a lemon, but I love the vinegar.

GENE: *(Moving furniture)* Help me, Blackie.

BLACKIE: What are you doing?

GENE: Making the corral.

ESTHER: Give me the white one, Emily, it needs a scrub.

JUNE: *(Resigned)* I'll be the red one.

EMILY: And I'm the blue elephant.

GENE: Let's get started! Start, June.

EMILY: Wait a minute. *(Solemnly)* We do this in memory of the drumfish. Goodbye, drumfish.

(They all trumpet. Normal voice:)

EMILY: Okay, June.

JUNE: Hi, big strong fellow.

GENE: Aw, you're just saying that.

JUNE: Nope. You look grand and tough to me. Say, why don't you come with me? Got a great place for ya.

GENE: Why not? It'd be my grand and tough pleasure to go with you.

JUNE: Here's our new home.

GENE: Looks a mite tiny to me.

JUNE: Soon you will love it, oh, giant one.

GENE: I've changed my mind.

JUNE: Oh, so sorry, my colossus ear, there is no changing of the mind.

EMILY: And so it came to pass that the Gene elephant was tamed.

GENE: Let me out! Hey! Hey! *(Throws himself into the furniture)*

JUNE: Are you tame yet, old fellow?

GENE: What'll it get me?

JUNE: You can go with me into the forest, and we will bring home another elephant.

GENE: Great, another elephant!

(GENE *and* JUNE *romp around and find* ESTHER.)

ESTHER: Hey Gene! How have you been? Long time no see.

GENE: Yeah. Like you to meet my friend, Red Elephant.

ESTHER: Oh, I'm always so happy to meet new elephants.

GENE: This place I'm living in is a real dump.

ESTHER: How exciting.

GENE: For some people that's exciting. For me, it's just a dump. Do you think you could come by and clean?

ESTHER: Gene, I'm never done cleaning the forest. I don't know when I could fit it in.

JUNE: This is a big job, White Elephant. Big. I think you'll love it.

ESTHER: I'll have a look.

(They romp to the corral, ESTHER between.)

ESTHER: You've overestimated the size of this job.

GENE: Oh, no, it needs lots of cleaning.

JUNE: It's a huge job, dear.

ESTHER: I don't want to go in there.

JUNE: Yes, you do, you do. *(Nudges her)*

GENE: It ain't so bad, White Elephant. Give it a try. *(Nudges her)*

ESTHER: All right, but only because you say so, Gene Elephant.

(ESTHER and GENE go into the corral.)

EMILY: And it came to pass that White Elephant was tamed.

BLACKIE: This is unsettling my calm. *(He takes a pill.)*

ESTHER: Boy, I sure am sad.

JUNE: What exactly is the problem?

ESTHER: You were wrong about the extent of this cleaning job.

JUNE: You need another elephant to clean up after.

ESTHER: That would help.

JUNE: Let's go find someone.

(The three romp around and find EMILY.)

EMILY: Hi guys, where've you been?

ESTHER: We've been living in a really clean place.

EMILY: I'm sorry to hear that. Why don't you come on back to the forest. The forest is always a mess.

ESTHER: Where I'm living is a pretty terrific place.

GENE: The terrificest.

ESTHER: Our pal and buddy, here, fixed it up for us to stay there.

EMILY: How do you do?

JUNE: Hi. I'll bet you'd love the place, Blue Elephant. Why don't you come and live with us?

EMILY: Thanks, Red Elephant, but I love it here. I don't think I could be happy anywhere else.

GENE: Too bad. This is it. Home. *(He pushes her into the corral.)*

EMILY: And it came to pass that Emily was tamed.

JUNE: Blue Elephant.

EMILY: Blue Elephant was tamed.

JUNE: How are my three friends today?

GENE: Crowded.

ESTHER: Clean.

EMILY: Blue.

JUNE: Well, we could all go for a romp, find another friend. Come on.

(The four romp around until they find BLACKIE.)

BLACKIE: What do I say?

GENE: Hello, Elephant.

BLACKIE: Hello, Elephant.

GENE: How you been?

BLACKIE: How you been?

GENE: I've been fine, how you been?

BLACKIE: I've been fine, how you been?

ESTHER: We've been living in a new place.

EMILY: It's cozy.

ESTHER: And clean.

GENE: Full of fun.

JUNE: You'd love it there, big guy.

EMILY: Perfect for you, Black Elephant.

BLACKIE: There are already so many of you.

GENE: The more the merrier.

ESTHER: What's one more among friends?

BLACKIE: I don't have friends.

JUNE: All elephants are friends of all other elephants.

EMILY: Come take a look at it.

GENE: It's a great place.

ESTHER: We want you to come with us.

JUNE: You have to come along with us.

(The four of them bully him toward the entrance of the corral.)

EMILY: See?

JUNE: Don't you think that's something?

ESTHER: So clean.

JUNE: A perfect fit.

EMILY: A fit for a king.

GENE: Get in.

BLACKIE: *(Breaks away from them, shouts)* No! Stay away. *(He holds them off with his elephant.)*

EMILY: That's not right. What are you doing?

BLACKIE: I don't know! Stay away from me.

EMILY: You have to go in. It's the game.

BLACKIE: No! I don't want to go in. *(He drops his elephant and starts to keen.)* Eeeeeeeeeeeeeeeeeeeeeeeeeeeeeeeeeee eeeee! *(Continues keening to the end of the scene.)*

EMILY: *(Pause)* What's he doing?

GENE: He's thinking.

EMILY: Why is he making that noise?

JUNE: Thinking hurts.

Scene Three

(A week later. The living room. A steady rain. JUNE enters from kitchen, followed by BLACKIE who is holding a small paintbrush.)

BLACKIE: Made of strings?

JUNE: *(Annoyed)* Yes, small strings. Extremely small. Unbelievably tiny…strings.

BLACKIE: And it's expanding?

JUNE: Of course. If it weren't, the night would be as bright as the day.

BLACKIE: Just hold it, hold it a minute, okay? The universe is made of strings. And the universe is expanding.

JUNE: That's right.

(GENE enters from upstairs, looks at them, looks in the corner where his fishing rod usually hangs. It isn't there.)

BLACKIE: So. Is the number of strings expanding, or is the size of the strings expanding?

JUNE: Neither.

BLACKIE: Then what's expanding?!

JUNE: The universe!

BLACKIE: You're leaving out steps, something.

JUNE: I'm not leaving out steps, you're just not making the proper leaps.

BLACKIE: What leaps?

JUNE: Leaps, leaps! You have to take some of this on faith and make leaps!

BLACKIE: You know what I think?! I think if you understood this, you could explain it better!

JUNE: I...think I'm going out for a walk.

BLACKIE: You shouldn't. Not without a good reason.

JUNE: I have a good reason, thank you. Goodbye, I love you.

BLACKIE: *(Pause)* Pardon me?

GENE: Just a minute, please. Where's my fishing gear?

BLACKIE: It's drying.

GENE: Drying from what?

BLACKIE: Paint.

GENE: You painted my fishing rod?

BLACKIE: Of course I painted it. It was all chipped.

GENE: You let him paint my fishing rod?

BLACKIE: *(Sarcastic)* Why not? It was a straight ahead task, no leaps required. She thought I could handle it.

GENE: I don't know who to kill first. Where is it?

BLACKIE: Kitchen.

(GENE *walks into the kitchen.*)

BLACKIE: Why shouldn't I have painted the fishing rod?

JUNE: Because you probably ruined it.

BLACKIE: Why didn't you tell me?

(GENE *reenters with a piece of cardboard covered with paint drippings.*)

GENE: What's this?

BLACKIE: It's a spot of paint.

GENE: I know it's a spot of paint, sport. What's it doing?

BLACKIE: (*Sighs. He takes the pill bottle from his pocket and takes one. He is testy.*) I don't know what you're talking about, I never know what you're talking about. It's a spot of paint, it's lying on the cardboard, what do you think it's doing?!

GENE: I'm curious to know how the paint on this cardboard got into this peculiar shape.

BLACKIE: (*Teeth clenched*) I don't know. I must have put my brush in it.

GENE: You mean, you painted? You made art?

BLACKIE: I suppose.

GENE: All right! Now we're talking. Get me the hammer and a couple of nails.

(BLACKIE *goes to kitchen.*)

GENE: Did you see this?

JUNE: Yes, I just don't happen to think it's that remarkable.

(BLACKIE *enters with hammer, etc.*)

GENE: Put this right here.

BLACKIE: No.

GENE: (*Surprised*) No?

BLACKIE: Put it here.

GENE: All right. (*Hangs picture*) What do you think?

BLACKIE: (*Taking another pill*) It makes me feel sick.

JUNE: Put your head between your knees and breathe deeply.

BLACKIE: Are you trying to fool me? Is she trying to fool me?

GENE: It's an accepted cure for art nausea.

BLACKIE: *(Head between knees)* There were arts in the place where I was before I was here.

GENE: In a vault?

BLACKIE: *(Head up)* How did you know that?

GENE: Lucky guess.

BLACKIE: You know so much.

JUNE: Oh brother.

BLACKIE: You know things I never heard of. You know how to fish.

GENE: You want to learn how to fish?

BLACKIE: Yes. …What am I saying!? I don't know. Maybe.

GENE: Get the rod.

BLACKIE: Yes, sir.

GENE: Don't call me sir.

BLACKIE: Yes… *(Sighs, takes pill, goes to kitchen)*

GENE: Thy rod and thy shaft they come for me. No. Thy rod on the raft it…

JUNE: Dad, he's making me crazy.

GENE: Yeah? Well, at least you know what's happening. He's feeling things he's never felt before, doesn't know why, and is taking C caplets to make it stop. Not easy for him, I'll tell you.

(BLACKIE *enters with rod.)*

GENE: Okay. *(Takes the rod)* We need a fish. *(Looks at* JUNE*)* Nah. Emily!!

EMILY: *(Offstage)* What?

GENE: *(Shouting)* Come down here.

(EMILY enters.)

EMILY: What do you want? Wow, look at that. Where'd that come from?

GENE: Artists Anonymous. *(Hands her the end of fishing line.)* Hold this.

EMILY: Why'd you paint your fishing rod? That was dumb.

GENE: Just hold. *(He starts to unwind the fishing line around the living room, wiping the paint off of the line.)*

JUNE: I'm going to go read.

BLACKIE: I thought you were going out.

JUNE: You were mistaken.

BLACKIE: I don't know why you read. It's all on video. You could watch a video.

JUNE: It isn't all on video.

BLACKIE: Everything important. With videos, everything is explained. What good is reading if you can't explain to me what you read? Strings!

JUNE: And what if you couldn't watch video? What if there were a power failure?

BLACKIE: There won't be another power failure.

JUNE: Sure, sure. That's what they said before. And now look at it—a zillion defrosted zygotes had to be sent through the space disposal, and nobody knows how to code new ones.

GENE: Almost nobody.

BLACKIE: You're the only one?

GENE: I hope so.

BLACKIE: Are you going to code?

EMILY: Not Gene! They treated him bad. Once they had a thousand years worth of people, they sent him away without so much as thank you.

BLACKIE: And that...annoyed you?

EMILY: You bet it annoyed him. They begged him to come back to the lab, they got down on their knees, but he told them they could just forget it.

JUNE: He did not. You didn't say that, did you? What did you tell them?

GENE: I didn't tell them anything.

JUNE: What do you mean you didn't tell them anything? You had to tell them something.

GENE: I must have missed the interview.

EMILY & JUNE: What!!

JUNE: You didn't go?!

GENE: I didn't have the time. (To BLACKIE) See, I have to fish. Fishing relaxes me so that I can put together the big plan. And I had to spend so much of that morning finding my boat that...well...

JUNE: You didn't even go?

BLACKIE: So if you had had your boat...?

GENE: Nearby say, in its old slip, see, I could have fished, thought through the problems, made the meeting. Figured out how to restore the lost catalogue of genetic engineering, taught a few tricks to the boys, and girl, at the lab...You want to fish?

BLACKIE: It's raining.

GENE: It's always raining. Take the rod.

BLACKIE: What do I do?

GENE: Reel it in. Emily, be a fish.

EMILY: *(Taking the line)* You didn't even go. I thought you told them no thanks buddy and you didn't even go.

BLACKIE: What do I do?

GENE: Pull back fast on the line to set the hook.

(BLACKIE *pulls hard on the line.*)

EMILY: Ouch, ouch!

JUNE: What?

EMILY: It cut my hand.

JUNE: Give me the line. *(She wraps something around her hand, then the line.)*

GENE: Look at that. Is she smart or what?

JUNE: I don't believe you didn't go.

GENE: This is gonna be tough, Blackie. It's a canny fish on the line.

JUNE: Just get on with it. *(She starts to walk backwards unfurling the fishing line.)*

BLACKIE: What do I do?

GENE: You get real excited and set the hook.

BLACKIE: I don't feel excited.

GENE: It grows on you.

(JUNE *lets go of the line.*)

BLACKIE: What did she do?

JUNE: I spit the hook!

BLACKIE: Why is she yelling?

GENE: She's a cantankerous fish. Ya gotta be more… gentle. You can't just jerk the line around. Take the bait again, Drumfish.

JUNE: Sure, sure, why not? It makes as much sense as anything else around here.

GENE: You feel a little pull on the line, but you're not sure what it is.

BLACKIE: But I can see she has it in her hand.

GENE: She's forty feet under water, sport.

(JUNE *grabs the line firmly and runs around the living room with the line.* BLACKIE *holds on.*)

JUNE: One day I'm an elephant, the next I'm a fish. Why not?!

GENE: Now you're sure what it is. Set the hook! Pull back on the line. There you go. Now you're fishing.

BLACKIE: She's pulling very hard.

JUNE: You might have told me, that you didn't go!

EMILY: You might have told me, too!

GENE: Just let her run. You don't want to break the line.

BLACKIE: All right. She's slowing down.

GENE: Yeah, she's starting to get tired. Reel it in a little. How's it feel?

BLACKIE: I think I'm pulling her in. No, she's running again. I let the line out a little, there she goes. She's getting tired. I pull the line in again. I slowly reel in the line. No! There she goes! She slows down. She's tired. I'm reeling her in! Here she comes!! She's coming in!! What do I do?!!!

GENE: When she's real close, hand me the rod and then grab her.

BLACKIE: All right! Here! Yaaaaa!

(BLACKIE *hands* GENE *the rod and lifts* JUNE *into his arms.*)

BLACKIE: *(Sings)* "He he he he heeeeeeeee!" *(He stops suddenly. An awkward pause)*

JUNE: Put me down.

BLACKIE: Certainly, Miss.

(JUNE *starts to go upstairs.*)

EMILY: Where you going, Fish?

JUNE: Uh… *(Points upstairs)* Up. *(Exits)*

BLACKIE: Singing…feels good.

GENE: Yeah.

BLACKIE: *(Looking after* JUNE*)* And fishing…is amazing.

GENE: Yeah.

BLACKIE: I never knew.

GENE: Nobody wants you to know, either.

(Enter ESTHER. *She is in a semi-catatonic state. It's as if she were sleep walking. She walks into the middle of the room, kneels on the rug, and starts to bang her head slowly against the floor.* JUNE *hears and enters from above.)*

EMILY: What are you doing? *(Pause)* What is she doing?

GENE: Take it easy, Emily.

EMILY: No! No, I won't take it easy. What is it? What's she doing? Mom!!!

*(*GENE *goes to* ESTHER, *kneels by her side and touches her gently, trying to stop the motion without startling* ESTHER. BLACKIE *puts his hand on* EMILY's *shoulder.)*

GENE: Esther? Sweetie?

EMILY: Mom?!

BLACKIE: I'm sorry, Miss Emily. I think it's the suicide.

END OF ACT ONE

ACT TWO

Scene One

(The interior of the house. Weeks later. JULIA *marches downstairs carrying the blue elephant;* EMILY *follows. A steady rain.)*

JULIA: *(Machine gun sounds)* Ta ta ta ta ta ta.

EMILY: *(Stumbles after)* Give that back! Give me that! You creep. You error-filled zygote! Eliminatable mutant!

JULIA: *(Continues to march around the room, shoots* EMILY *with the elephant)* Bang! Bang, bang, bang, bang!

EMILY: Oh, brother. Put it down, Julia. You're making yourself completely ridiculous.

JULIA: I don't have to. You said I could play with it.

EMILY: Play with it, not shoot with it.

JULIA: Let's play Eliminator.

EMILY: I'm sick of being in the sack.

JULIA: Let me try on your false foot.

EMILY: It won't fit you.

JULIA: Sure it will. Go get it.

EMILY: Oh, brother. *(Exits upstairs)*

JULIA: *(Shouts)* Blackie!

BLACKIE: *(Enters from the kitchen)* Yes, Miss?

JULIA: Those pictures you took were useless. There weren't any people in them.

BLACKIE: If I take pictures with people in them, the people will know I am taking pictures of them.

JULIA: Oh. Huh. But, see. You got to get pictures of them doing eliminatable offenses; proof that Gene is not going back to the lab. Then, zappo, wacko, all of them, through the space disposal. (*She uses the elephant to make battle gestures.*)

EMILY: (*Enters from upstairs*) What are you doing with that? You don't know how to play at all.

JULIA: Let me have your foot.

EMILY: Here. I don't think you're going to like it. You can loosen the straps if you need to.

BLACKIE: Can I help you, Miss?

JULIA: I can figure it out myself. Help me with this.

(BLACKIE *fastens on the foot. She gets up and walks around.*)

EMILY: (*Picks up the elephant*) Hello, Blue. We didn't mean to play shooting with you. It was a horrible mistake, one we're sad to have maked.

JULIA: Hush up. Call me Emily, zygote mutant with a goofy foot. Ouch, this hurts. I don't like this at all. Take it off me, Blackie.

(ESTHER *comes downstairs. She is in her catatonic state. She goes into the kitchen.* JULIA *does not see,* EMILY *and* BLACKIE *do.*)

EMILY: You should go home now.

JULIA: I can stay as long as I want to.

EMILY: Your elders might get mad.

JULIA: That's ridiculous.

EMILY: I want you to go!

JULIA: I don't care what you want. I'm going to stay…
unless…you give me this blue elephant.

EMILY: Take him, just go!

JULIA: *(Surprised)* I can take him?

EMILY: Just get out of here. You're unsettling my calm.

JULIA: Then give me two.

EMILY: No!

JULIA: Why not?

EMILY: Just get out!

JULIA: No, not unless you give me two elephants.

EMILY: Some friend you are.

JULIA: I'm the best friend you ever had.

(ESTHER *comes in. She slowly walks to the middle of the
room and lays face down on the carpet. She doesn't move.)*

EMILY: Esther? Get up.

JULIA: *(Pause)* Your female elder is lying down with her
face in the rug.

EMILY: I know.

JULIA: *(Pause)* What's she doing?

EMILY: Resting. Esther? Go up to bed. It's time for your
nap.

JULIA: She takes naps?

EMILY: You gotta go home.

JULIA: No, I don't.

EMILY: You can take the elephants.

JULIA: All of them?

EMILY: Yes, take them, take them all.

JULIA: Are you trying to get rid of me?

(ESTHER *rises to her knees and starts to bang her head into the floor. She does this slowly but with a fierce determination.*)

EMILY: Stop it! You'll hurt yourself. (*To* JULIA) Will you get out of here?!

JULIA: You haven't given me all my elephants.

EMILY: Take your stupid elephants. Just go home. (*Whispering*) Mom, cut it out.

(ESTHER *freezes.*)

BLACKIE: Perhaps I should take her upstairs.

(BLACKIE *picks her up. She maintains her position. He carries her upstairs.*)

EMILY: I'll help you.

(EMILY *limps along behind.* JULIA *is left alone in the living room. She runs to her satchel which is lying on the living room floor, and gets out a container of dirt. She makes sure no one is coming downstairs. She throws dirt on the rug. She rubs the dirt in with her shoes.* BLACKIE *comes down the stairs.* JULIA *momentarily tries to hide what she has done.*)

JULIA: Oh, it's you again. Do you have any more film for me?

BLACKIE: (*Lying for the first time*) No.

JULIA: I wish we had a picture of that. (*Indicating upstairs*) What were you doing with her?

BLACKIE: Putting her to bed.

(EMILY *watches, unseen, at the top of the stairs.*)

JULIA: Why?

BLACKIE: It seemed the thing to do.

JULIA: Has she done this before?

BLACKIE: (*Lying*) Oh, no, never.

JULIA: Well, it looks like the suicide to me.

BLACKIE: She's a bit young for that.

JULIA: No, she isn't. My female elder's been Stage Three for half a year. Shopping. Obsessive shopping. You're not supposed to touch them. You're supposed to leave them alone until they snap. "There's nothing more useless than a woman over fifty except..."

BLACKIE: "...a man over sixty." I know this, Miss Julia. And I'll leave her alone when the time comes. It isn't the time yet.

JULIA: Then what was she doing with her face in the rug?

BLACKIE: *(Lying gets easier)* She was looking for dirt.

JULIA: That close?

BLACKIE: Yes. I've seen Miss Esther look for dirt with a magnifying glass.

JULIA: Has Gene said anything about going back to the lab?

BLACKIE: I don't think so.

JULIA: Why not? He got his boat back.

BLACKIE: I don't know.

JULIA: He'll never go back. We should just zap him now.

BLACKIE: *(Lying is great)* The problems are... complicated. Gene can't complete the entire lost catalogue of genetic engineering in a couple of weeks.

JULIA: Why are you calling him Gene?

BLACKIE: Mister Gene. Mister Gene. Mister Gene. I'm sorry, Miss!

JULIA: Well, calm down.

(BLACKIE takes a pill.)

JULIA: You better finish here and come back to our house.

BLACKIE: You have a new Blackie.

JULIA: He's a creep. He tells everything I do. Do you tell on Emily?

BLACKIE: She doesn't do anything to report.

JULIA: They're all a bunch of useless eliminatables. I'm going to get the elephants. Go get my coat.

(EMILY *disappears from the top of the stairs.* JULIA *goes upstairs.* BLACKIE *takes a camera out of his pocket and exposes the film, returns film and camera to his pocket. He hears* JULIA *returning with the elephants and goes to the closet for her coat.)*

JULIA: Wow, these are really heavy.

BLACKIE: Why don't you leave some of them here?

JULIA: No, I won't leave any of them. They're mine and they're going to my house. I only have to carry them to the stretch. Help me, Blackie.

BLACKIE: Why? You're doing fine, Miss.

JULIA: I am? Oh. Okay. Have some film for me next time. *(She exits with her satchel and the elephants.)* I'll be back.

BLACKIE: *(To the empty room)* And I'll be waiting for you.

EMILY: *(At the top of the stairs)* Who you talking to, Blackie?

BLACKIE: To Miss Julia, Miss.

EMILY: I don't see anybody.

BLACKIE: She is faster than the speed of sound.

EMILY: Hey, a joke.

BLACKIE: Thank you.

EMILY: You lied to her.

BLACKIE: I couldn't have.

EMILY: Yeah, you did. You said you'd never seen Mom like that before. You said we didn't talk about June's work in the lab.

BLACKIE: Did I say that?

EMILY: Yep. You said it.

BLACKIE: Fancy that.

EMILY: Blackies can't lie.

BLACKIE: Blackies do what they are told to do.

EMILY: Nobody told you to lie. Leastways, nobody here told you to lie.

BLACKIE: I told myself to lie.

EMILY: You can do that?

BLACKIE: You saw.

EMILY: Wow.

BLACKIE: She took the elephants.

EMILY: It doesn't matter.

BLACKIE: How is Miss…Mom?

EMILY: Did I call her that?

BLACKIE: Once or twice.

EMILY: *(Really sad)* She's really bad.

BLACKIE: I'm sorry.

EMILY: Yeah. *(She exits to the kitchen.)*

(BLACKIE is alone. He sits down to review the situation. ESTHER enters in a lucid state, sits on the stairs.)

ESTHER: It's me.

(BLACKIE stands quickly.)

ESTHER: Oh, sit down.

BLACKIE: How are you feeling, Miss?

ESTHER: Don't call me "Miss."

BLACKIE: I need to call you all "Miss." I need to lump you all together in the big female stew I keep simmering in my brain.

ESTHER: What!?

BLACKIE: I don't know what made me say that!! *(Pause, sigh, takes a handful of pills)* You feel better?

ESTHER: Sure. Where's Gene?

BLACKIE: Out.

ESTHER: If I'm not here when he gets back, tell him I said goodbye I love you. *(Pause)* I didn't think it would be like this. Gene said things were going to be different for us.

BLACKIE: How can they be different for you than they are for everybody?

ESTHER: He took away my stoppers. World turned upside down, and it wasn't too bad. Sex?

BLACKIE: No. Never.

ESTHER: They said sex was a dead drive. Without stoppers it's rockets and exploding kiwis.

BLACKIE: Kiwi? Beast?

ESTHER: Fruit. Very dark green interior with black spots. And our children would be our children.

BLACKIE: No!

ESTHER: Sure enough.

BLACKIE: But how…?

ESTHER: I was already pregnant when I requested my implants. Gene told them he would do the implantation himself. Back then when Gene wanted something, everybody jumped. The lab zygotes went through the Space Disposal.

BLACKIE: That's why Miss Emily is not perfect.

ESTHER: When Gene saw her little mangled foot, he wrapped her in a sheet and whisked us home to safety. Reported it later as an injury.

BLACKIE: And that's why Miss June works in a lab.

ESTHER: Yep. She showed the brains early.

BLACKIE: And they look like you.

ESTHER: Everybody in this family looks like Gene. I look like Gene. You look a little like him yourself.

BLACKIE: I do not!

ESTHER: You will. He's an unbridled force in nature. He told me our children would love us. I thought he'd lost his whole mind. I guess you didn't have elders.

BLACKIE: No. Group-house. Why did he do those things?

ESTHER: He didn't want to watch me die like this. He thought if we changed enough stuff, I wouldn't. What's that?

BLACKIE: What?

ESTHER: On the rug!

BLACKIE: It's common household dirt.

ESTHER: How do I usually deal with that?

BLACKIE: Vacuum cleaner.

ESTHER: I never used to clean; it's so pointless. Then, Stage Three and I turned into a stain remover.

BLACKIE: Isn't there something Gene can do?

ESTHER: I guess not. I'm not like the girls. I'm coded. *(Proudly)* I'm an eight.

BLACKIE: I thought you must be at least an eight.

ESTHER: Sure. An eight that's genetically coded to self-destruct any minute.

BLACKIE: Maybe Miss June could make something in the lab. Some pill.

ESTHER: I need something new.

BLACKIE: A pill. Try one of these.

ESTHER: I don't want one of those.

BLACKIE: They help me. *(Pause)* They used to help me.

ESTHER: Haven't done much for you lately, though, have they?

(Enter EMILY from kitchen. BLACKIE contemplates his pills.)

EMILY: You're up. Yeah!

ESTHER: Come here, Emily.

(They hug.)

EMILY: Julia took the elephants.

ESTHER: Fine. Let her family play the Taming game ninety-three times a week.

BLACKIE: *(Contemplates his pills)* They won't be capable of it.

ESTHER: Well, it's not like it's hard.

BLACKIE: They find any kind of extemporaneous dialogue difficult.

EMILY: Blackie lied to Julia.

ESTHER: Blackies can't lie.

(Enter JUNE from outside. She and BLACKIE stare at each other. He goes to the kitchen.)

EMILY: Do you two hate each other, or what?

JUNE: I need to talk to Dad. Emergency.

EMILY: Mom laid down on the rug again.

ESTHER: What have you got all over yourself?

JUNE: Protoplasmic swill.

EMILY: Have a little laboratory accident?

JUNE: Accident on purpose. They're trying to clone Dad!

EMILY: Isn't one of him enough?

JUNE: Oh, this is a whole new approach. If Dad won't come in and genetically code zygotes, they'll make a clone of Dad to do it.

EMILY: That's really stupid.

JUNE: Of course it's stupid. But they're going to try it. And if they think they're close to a clone, we're duck soup.

EMILY: Where'd they get Dad's cells?

JUNE: They got bits and pieces of Dad stashed from here to Timbuktu. They brought me these cells in a petri dish. "Thaw these cells," they said. I knew it was Dad. I checked the helix and it was him, sure enough.

ESTHER: Those are your father's cells?

JUNE: Yes.

ESTHER: *(To* JUNE*)* Come here. *(To* JUNE*'s soaked clothes)* Hi, there. Hi, sweetie.

JUNE: Oh, Mom.

(Enter GENE. *He is carrying a fish. He is in a slicker.)*

GENE: Esther, look, look what I got. "Hee hee hee hee heeeee!"

EMILY: Not now!

JUNE: Dad, there was an Inspector Mobile at the lab, today…

GENE: I'm trying to sing.

JUNE: And suddenly, the lab director shows up with these cells for me to thaw...your cells, you!

EMILY: Dad, Mom laid down on the rug—

JUNE: Dad, please come back to the lab.

ESTHER: Hi, there, Sweetie. Hi, there.

JUNE: Genetically code a frog or two. Keep them happy.

EMILY: I had to give Julia my elephants—

JUNE: You won't have to really code people, as long as they think you're trying—

EMILY: It took me one whole month to find stuff for those elephants.

JUNE: Please, stop with the elephants. Dad! If they think they've got your clone, they'll eliminate you!

EMILY: And it took me another whole month to make them.

JUNE: Dad, if you won't come to the lab, at least tell me what to do.

(BLACKIE *bursts into the living room. He is holding his bottle of pills.*)

BLACKIE: What have you done to my chemicals!?

GENE: Esther, remember how we clean these?

ESTHER: Hi there. Hi.

(GENE *cleans the fish.*)

GENE: Bluefish! I caught a drum, too. Threw him back. Didn't tell him he was supposed to be extinct. "Go out and mate!" I said.

BLACKIE: I demand to know what you have done...

GENE: Demand? La de da de da de da.

BLACKIE: What have you done to my chemicals?

GENE: How about this fish? It's for Esther.

BLACKIE: My pills. You're a renegade scientist. Miss Esther told me everything. I think you've been altering my chemicals. My brain is exploding. I AM NOT CALM!

GENE: *(Scales the fish)* I can see that.

BLACKIE: My pills!

JUNE: Oh, tell him.

GENE: Those pills prevent scurvy and promote healthy gums. Remember this, Esther? We scale first. Like this.

JUNE: Did you hear what I said about the lab?

GENE: No. It hurt my brain.

JUNE: The Inspectors are forcing us to clone. They want to clone you.

GENE: Those rascals.

JUNE: Tell me what to do. What if we produce a successful clone?

GENE: *(Continues to gut fish)* So what if they clone me? They're my clones. They're little me's. Little me's aren't going to cooperate.

EMILY: You cooperated for thirty years.

GENE: But I was almost ready to stop!

(Brief pause)

BLACKIE: I'm dying!

JUNE: No, you're not! You're not dying. Gene changed them the day you got here, and you're not dead.

BLACKIE: I will die without my pills.

GENE: You can get more pills.

BLACKIE: I can?

GENE: Sure. But you don't have to if you don't want to.

BLACKIE: I don't…have to…

GENE: Yeah. If you don't, the possibilities loom.

(BLACKIE *doesn't move until he speaks again.*)

JUNE: *(Sarcastic)* You're such a revolutionary.

EMILY: Mom laid down in the rug again today. She froze solid as a rock. Blackie carried her upstairs, and I had to give Julia my elephants so she'd go away.

GENE: *(To* ESTHER*)* What's going on?

ESTHER: Hi…there…hi.

GENE: Esther, honey? Remember the fish? You and me on the Proud Esther. You caught them, I cleaned them, you cooked them. Remember fish scales? You used to hold them up to the light. Said they looked like little stars. Little daylight stars.

ESTHER: Hi there. Hi. Hello. *(She goes upstairs.)*

GENE: *(Very very sad)* Oh, boy.

EMILY: Dad. Is it Stage Four?

GENE: Do you know how many…millions…of…people I coded to do this? Somebody clean up the mess. *(Follows* ESTHER *upstairs)*

(Pause, then EMILY *starts to pick up the mess.)*

EMILY: Blackie, wanna help?

BLACKIE: I don't…have to. If I don't…want to.

Scene Two

(Three weeks later. The living room. BLACKIE *in the outfit of a Native American Indian; feathers, bare chest, etc, enters making attack sounds.* EMILY *follows, making the same sounds. A steady rain.)*

EMILY: I gotta rest. *(She plops in a chair.)*

BLACKIE: All right. *(He exits to the kitchen.)*

EMILY: Hey. Where are you going? Blackie? I just want to rest for a minute. I still want to play. Come on back.

BLACKIE: *(Enters with a large pot)* We'll rest properly. *(He puts the pot on the floor, looks around, picks up a book and tears it up, and puts the pieces in the pot. Sets it on fire)*

EMILY: Campfire?

BLACKIE: Campfire.

EMILY: *(She gets up.)* You burned a book.

BLACKIE: Fuel.

EMILY: You burned a book. Wow!

BLACKIE: Many books have burned.

EMILY: Not in this house. What book was it?

BLACKIE: I don't know. Sit down and rest. Tell me more.

EMILY: Where did I leave off?

BLACKIE: Black men roamed the continent. Black men ruled the continent. The black man was king.

EMILY: Yeah. Okay. Long long ago, in the time of the elephant and before the nuclear reactor and the steady rain, white men lived across the ocean and the black man was king of the continent. He lived with the elephants. He rode wild animals, and he fished for the mighty drumfish.

BLACKIE: Like Gene caught.

EMILY: Yeah, only there were lots of them.

BLACKIE: And no man in the land was mightier than he.

EMILY: I never said that.

BLACKIE: You implied it. The black man walked the unpaved land of the land. No one gave him his daily instructions or told him to take his chemicals. The black man hunted beasts which he cooked and ate. He was free. He lived alone in his tepee. What's a tepee, again?

EMILY: It's the big rubber sheet. With the sticks to hold it up.

BLACKIE: It must not have been very comfortable.

EMILY: Times were tough.

BLACKIE: The black man lived alone in his tepee. And hunted the mighty beasts, and drumfish and ate...kiwi.

EMILY: He lived with his family.

BLACKIE: What?

EMILY: He didn't have to live alone, oh mighty one. He lived with his wife. And their children.

BLACKIE: What wife?

EMILY: His wife!

BLACKIE: They had women?

EMILY: How else did they have itty bitty ones?

BLACKIE: You said only the *black* men lived here. All the rest lived across the ocean.

EMILY: The white people lived across the ocean. The black men and the black women and the black babies lived here.

BLACKIE: *(Pause)* Black...women?

(EMILY sighs in exasperation.)

BLACKIE: You are saying there were black...women?

EMILY: Sure. I mean, I guess.

BLACKIE: What happened to them?

EMILY: I don't know. I guess they're extinct.

BLACKIE: *(Very very sad)* I should very much like to see a black woman.

EMILY: I'm sorry, Blackie. What should I do?

BLACKIE: I don't know. There's a hole spreading in my chest. This must be death.

EMILY: You're just lonely. We all get lonely. Even Dad.

BLACKIE: Black women. I never knew.

EMILY: What did they tell you?

BLACKIE: Nothing! Do you understand? They tell us nothing! We learn what we learn!

EMILY: What did you think? I mean you must have thought something.

BLACKIE: I didn't think anything. Until now!

EMILY: Dad says that's why they erased history. So there wouldn't be any comparisons. So people wouldn't ask questions. He didn't ask questions for years. Then he asked a lot of them. But nobody answered.

BLACKIE: *(Holds his head)* My brain is exploding.

EMILY: You really look fierce, Blackie.

BLACKIE: Don't call me that!

EMILY: Fierce?

BLACKIE: Don't call me Blackie.

EMILY: Okay. Pick another name. We all picked our names.

BLACKIE: You *picked* your names?

EMILY: Sure.

BLACKIE: Then why did you pick such dumb ones?!

EMILY: *(Hurt)* They aren't dumb. They're our names and we picked them. You're really nasty. I'm not gonna play with you anymore. You're just a big creep. *(Exits to upstairs)*

(BLACKIE *is alone for a moment. Filled with regret or something like it.* JUNE *enters from outside. They are embarrassed.)*

JUNE: Uh... Hi. Great outfit. What's burning?

BLACKIE: Emily and I made a campfire.

JUNE: Oh. Why's it so quiet?

(BLACKIE *doesn't answer.)*

JUNE: How's Mom?!

BLACKIE: She's horrible! How do you expect her to be?! She wasn't even interested in a formula for getting cat piss out of upholstery. She doesn't care anymore.

JUNE: This is all Dad's fault. He led her to expect a different end. I should have realized. She's a coded eight. It's what they do.

BLACKIE: Dad does what he can.

JUNE: Don't you call him Dad.

BLACKIE: He tried. It might have led to a different conclusion.

JUNE: Some day when we're not watching closely enough, she'll jump into the bay.

BLACKIE: You spout video pessimism as if you were an Inspector's daughter.

JUNE: I do not spout. I do not spout pessimism. It's how it is. I want us to get by. I want what's best for my family. I am not going to dance around in Dad's dream.

BLACKIE: *(Pause)* I dreamed last night.

JUNE: Oh. You get them after you've been off stoppers.

BLACKIE: I thought I had been watching a video. But they don't make videos like this.

JUNE: What was it about?

BLACKIE: *(Embarrassed)* I...

JUNE: You don't have to... Dreams are private. Did it make you happy?

BLACKIE: It did. And then it made me profoundly sad.

JUNE: This is just the beginning. Wait until you feel lonely.

BLACKIE: I already felt lonely.

JUNE: How do you know?

BLACKIE: Emily diagnosed it. I thought it was only death.

JUNE: We all get it. You can learn from it.

BLACKIE: Learn? My mind is exploding.

JUNE: Do you want pills? I can get you stoppers.

BLACKIE: I don't know.

JUNE: Me and Emily never took stoppers. Well, actually, I did. I just didn't tell Mom and Dad.

BLACKIE: What did you think of them?

JUNE: They were great.

BLACKIE: Then why did you stop?

JUNE: You wouldn't understand.

BLACKIE: *(Sarcastic)* No. Nobody can understand anything difficult except June the loon scientific raccoon.

JUNE: I'm sorry. I didn't like being like everybody else.

BLACKIE: I understand.

JUNE: I'm sorry. I forget that you're not like everybody else.

BLACKIE: You forget that everybody isn't like everybody else.

JUNE: Why are you picking on me? Why does everybody pick on me?

BLACKIE: *(A fact)* I guess you're everyone's least favorite person.

JUNE: Ah… You… What…I'm the only female in the whole lab. They look at me like I'm a bug. I eat my lunch alone. I work at a table by myself. I worry about Mom. I worry about Dad. I'm terrified that they're gonna take Emily away some day and I won't even know about it. Why…

BLACKIE: What are you doing?

JUNE: I…

BLACKIE: Is something wrong with your eyes?

JUNE: Leave my eyes alone. They're just crying.

BLACKIE: Can you stop them? It is very unpleasant to watch.

JUNE: If I could stop them I would stop them!

BLACKIE: Is there something I can do?

JUNE: They'll stop. I'll hold my head. They'll stop. *(She wraps her arms around her head.)*

BLACKIE: Here. I'll do that. *(He wraps his arms around her head.)* Is this right?

JUNE: Yeah. Don't squeeze though.

BLACKIE: I know not to squeeze. I'm not going to break your head. *(Pause)* You were in my dream. You were a fish, well, I guess we all were. We lived at the bottom of the water. We moved through the water, we floated.

JUNE: I fly in my dreams.

BLACKIE: We floated. It was warm. We lived in caves at the bottom of the water. You wanted to swim fast. To race. I raced you.

JUNE: Who won?

BLACKIE: I woke up.

JUNE: *(Pause)* My eyes are okay now.

BLACKIE: Should I…let go of your head?

JUNE: Maybe you should wait another couple of seconds.

BLACKIE: *(Brief pause)* I told Julia's Blackie to stop taking stoppers.

JUNE: *(Slowly disentangles herself)* You what?!

BLACKIE: I told him I had stopped. I proved it by singing the Gene tune. He was very impressed. I told him to tell others.

JUNE: You can't do that! Have you lost your whole mind?

BLACKIE: You're in charge of the chemicals, aren't you?

JUNE: You know I am. Don't change the subject!

BLACKIE: You distribute the stoppers, yes?

JUNE: My lab does, yes.

BLACKIE: Make fake stoppers. Like you gave me. Put them in the bottles marked "Life-sustaining chemicals, Blackies Only."

JUNE: I won't do that! That's instant elimination.

BLACKIE: For breaking the rules?

JUNE: Yes. For breaking the rules.

BLACKIE: Your family breaks rules every day.

JUNE: That's different.

BLACKIE: Because the rules you break don't do any good?

JUNE: What!?

BLACKIE: Do something with your knowledge. Do something that matters. Do something dangerous.

JUNE: I risk my neck every day to keep those nits in the lab from cloning Gene. Gene risks his life every time he sets foot in that little boat. Emily could be eliminated by any twit who finds her limp offensive. Just what do you know about danger?

BLACKIE: I know that you could do more. You could help more.

JUNE: We'd be right through the Space Disposal.

BLACKIE: If Gene doesn't help them, they're going to sack you. If Gene does help them, they're going to sack you. Why not do something really big. Make fake stoppers. Distribute them to Blackies.

JUNE: Give me one reason why I should.

BLACKIE: *(Thinks up a reason)* Because once Blackies are off stoppers, the Inspectors will have new problems. The Inspectors will be distracted from "Gene and his family." Make fake stoppers.

JUNE: I'd have to keep them separate. Separate them from the ones everybody else takes.

BLACKIE: Could you do that?

JUNE: Yeah. Yeah. I could…

BLACKIE: How long will it take?

JUNE: Not too long. A couple of weeks.

BLACKIE: Do it. Let the mighty black warrior rise again.

JUNE: Who? Ohhh. Emily's history game.

BLACKIE: Yes. We are playing the history of black men.

JUNE: Well, don't take it too literally. Emily learned from Dad, and who can tell if Dad remembered it right in the first place.

BLACKIE: Emily said there were black women. Is that true?

JUNE: There was a whole black race. The women were genetically eliminated.

BLACKIE: What was wrong with them?

JUNE: Nothing.

BLACKIE: W...Why...?

JUNE: Some scientific fast fix. I don't really know why.

BLACKIE: Did you ever see...

JUNE: I never saw a black woman.

BLACKIE: What...were they like?

JUNE: Like me. But black.

(Silence)

GENE: *(From kitchen)* Why is it so quiet? *(Pause)* Somebody! Helloooo! *(He enters.)* Hi. Nice outfit. What's that!!!? Who's been here?

JUNE: What is it?

GENE: A burned book.

JUNE: Oh, no!

GENE: Who did this?

BLACKIE: I did it.

JUNE: You used a book for your campfire? A book?

GENE: *Dr Halloran's Complete Window Box.* This is a book about plants. What did plants ever do to you?

BLACKIE: The once noble black man roaming North America paused by the campfire to rest and tell stories.

JUNE: You don't burn books for fuel.

BLACKIE: *(Sarcastic)* Sorry. Were you planning on doing some gardening this spring?

GENE: Emily let you do this?

BLACKIE: I didn't ask her.

GENE: Oh. Where is she?

BLACKIE: She is busy being sad in her room.

GENE: What did I do? I wasn't even here.

BLACKIE: You're not the only one capable of inflicting pain. I said her name was dumb.

GENE: You're right. We all have dumb names.

BLACKIE: I want a name.

GENE: Take mine.

BLACKIE: I want a great black chief's name. Do you know any?

GENE: Let me see. A-B-C-D-E-F-G-H-I-J-K-L-M…M-M-M. Starts with M. Mar…this is a long time ago. Mal…Mo, Morris! Morris something. I can't remember. Morris.

BLACKIE: Call me Morris.

JUNE: Morris.

GENE: Morris. Rhymes with Horace. Good choice.

BLACKIE: You're sure this is the name of a great black leader?

GENE: Oh, yeah. I'm positive. Emily!

EMILY: *(Offstage)* Leave me alone.

GENE: Get down here. We got an emergency.

JUNE: You're just going to scare her.

EMILY: Mom! *(Enters)* Is it Mom? Is Mom okay?

JUNE: *(To* GENE*)* I told you.

GENE: Blackie's got a new name.

(GENE *exits to bedrooms.*)

EMILY: What is it?

BLACKIE: Morris.

EMILY: Talk about dumb names.

BLACKIE: He was a great black leader in the time of black women.

EMILY: *(Into it)* Yeah? Oh, wow. That's great.

(EMILY goes to the kitchen. GENE enters leading ESTHER.)

GENE: Esther, Esther, we're going to rename Blackie.

ESTHER: New name?

GENE: Do I see a flicker of interest?

ESTHER: Little.

GENE: Great!

BLACKIE: I am Morris. Named for a great black leader from the time of black women.

ESTHER: He dress like that?

BLACKIE: Yes, he did.

ESTHER: Nice.

JUNE: But he didn't burn books.

BLACKIE: At least he used them for something!

GENE: Start it, Esther.

ESTHER: *(Shakes BLACKIE's hand)* How do you do, Morris? Morris, I'd like you to meet June.

JUNE: How do you do, Morris? I'd like you to meet Gene.

GENE: How do you do, Morris? I'd like you to meet Emily.

(BLACKIE turns to meet EMILY, she enters from the kitchen and throws a bucket of water on him.)

BLACKIE: Ahhhhh! Why...did you do that?!

EMILY: We always do that.

BLACKIE: That was reprehensible.

EMILY: That was cold water.

BLACKIE: I...I don't believe this.

JUNE: Ooo. I forgot about the water.

GENE: It's been years.

BLACKIE: Why did you do that?

GENE: It's completely obvious.

JUNE: Go dry off so you don't get sick.

BLACKIE: I won't get sick! Don't tell me what to do!

EMILY: Oooo. I remember how I felt. I felt mad, too. It was great.

GENE: It was pretty great.

BLACKIE: This is not great!

EMILY: Bet you don't feel lonely anymore.

BLACKIE: *(Surprised)* No. I don't feel lonely. Can I have a towel?

JUNE: *(Exiting)* Allow me.

BLACKIE: Gene, what's going to happen?

GENE: Read a few books. You'll know what's going to happen.

BLACKIE: Is the human race going to end?

GENE: Nothing's going to end. No more lab-concocted people.

BLACKIE: What will happen?!!?

GENE: Back to natural selection.

BLACKIE: What does that mean??!!?

(Enter JUNE with towel.)

EMILY: You're getting awful loud, Blackie.

BLACKIE: Morris!!

EMILY: Morris.

GENE: Natural selection means it's catch as catch can with sperms and eggs.

JUNE: No more Inspectors. No more Eliminators. Just boys and girls and natural selection.

BLACKIE: What will happen to Blackies?

GENE: They'll become part of the genetic pool. No reason why not once the stoppers are gone. You could breed now. You could breed with…June.

JUNE: Dad!

ESTHER: Grandchildren…?

EMILY: Nieces and nephews!

GENE: Eight weeks off stoppers. Hasn't Lieutenant Pecker stood up and saluted yet?

BLACKIE: …Excuse me. *(Starts to go upstairs)*

GENE: Where you off to?

BLACKIE: Getting dressed. *(He starts to go upstairs, turns.)* She is not a black woman. *(He exits.)*

ESTHER: Grandchildren.

JUNE: *(To* ESTHER*)* He doesn't like me.

EMILY: I think you embarrassed him, Dad.

JUNE: *(To* GENE*)* He doesn't like me.

GENE: Don't worry. You're geographically correct.

ESTHER: *(Goes to* JUNE *and shakes her)* Grandchildren!

GENE: Are you saying you want grandchildren, Esther?

ESTHER: You bet I want grandchildren!

GENE: What about the suicide?

ESTHER: Don't be ridiculous, Gene. *(Growing happier and happier)* Grandchildren!

(JUNE starts to exit the house.)

GENE: A new start. Where are you going?

JUNE: I don't know. I...I...need something.

ESTHER: You won't find it out there. You're blushing! You're a blushing bride! Grandchildren!

(They all gather around JUNE.)

EMILY: Oh good, we get to think up a new game! One with rings! Rings!

JUNE: I don't want...I don't think I want to...he doesn't like me!

ESTHER: Yes, he does, he does.

EMILY: What's geographically correct?

GENE: The bedroom next door.

ESTHER: *(Pokes JUNE in the arm)* Exploding kiwis!!

Scene Three

(The living room, months later. Enter BLACKIE carrying GENE's fishing rod. GENE follows wearing his slicker. A steady rain)

GENE: Give me that!

BLACKIE: Keep your voice down! You can't go.

GENE: I'm going.

BLACKIE: Are you in, or not? You have to help us!

GENE: I don't have to help anyone!

BLACKIE: If you're not helping us you're helping them.

GENE: *(Pause)* Where do you come up with these things?

BLACKIE: Emily is in charge of slogans.

GENE: I'm going fishing. Give me my rod.

BLACKIE: Aren't you going to say, "Goodbye, I love you"?

GENE: Goodbye, I love you.

BLACKIE: Not to me!

GENE: Listen, Morris, I won't code zygotes for you, them, George Washington, anybody. Sorry.

BLACKIE: That's not what... Who?

(GENE *takes the rod and exits.* BLACKIE *puts on a slicker and exits. Enter* JULIA *and* EMILY *from upstairs, carrying elephants.*)

JULIA: Why don't you make some new ones so I don't have to bring them back every time?

EMILY: Why don't you leave them here?

JULIA: Because they're mine.

EMILY: Okay, they're yours. Leave them here. No one will touch them.

(*Enter* ESTHER. *Knitting, humming* Mule Skinner Blues)

ESTHER: Hello. The elephants again? Why don't you leave them here if you're going to bring them back every day?

JULIA: (*Points to* EMILY) That's what she said.

ESTHER: Well, why don't you?

JULIA: Because they're mine!

ESTHER: Ah, they're yours. I see.

JULIA: Here. This is for you. (*She takes a handful of dirt from her pocket and scatters it on the rug.*)

ESTHER: Oh, my. That's an interesting design. Thank you, dear.

JULIA: Julia. My name is Julia.

ESTHER: Thank you, Julia.

JULIA: Aren't you going to clean it up?

ESTHER: Clean what up?

JULIA: That, that!

ESTHER: No. I don't think so. *(She sits, knits, hums.)*

JULIA: What's she doing?

ESTHER: Knitting.

JULIA: What's that noise?

ESTHER: I don't hear any noise.

JULIA: It's not singing, is it?

ESTHER: Singing?

JULIA: Yes, singing! What's the matter with all you people?!

EMILY: Nothing's the matter with us.

(ESTHER hums.)

JULIA: Is she singing or not?

EMILY: *(Listens to* ESTHER*)* Asthma.

JULIA: Where's Blackie?

EMILY: I don't know.

JULIA: *(Shouts)* Blackie!

ESTHER: Great lungs. *(She starts upstairs.)*

*(*BLACKIE *enters from outside, damp.* ESTHER *hold up her knitting for him to see.* ESTHER *exits.)*

JULIA: What were you doing out there?

BLACKIE: Weeds.

JULIA: Weeds? You weren't talking to my Blackie, were you? That's not allowed.

BLACKIE: Weeds.

JULIA: *(To* EMILY*)* Get another one of my elephants out of the stretch so Blackie can play, too.

EMILY: Maybe he doesn't want to play.

JULIA: Who cares what he wants? Get another elephant.

EMILY: Okay. *(She puts on a slicker and goes outside.)*

JULIA: Everything's getting really weird in this house. I used to like to come here and spy. Now it's too creepy.

BLACKIE: It seems perfectly normal to me.

JULIA: Well you're pretty creepy yourself. So's my Blackie. He doesn't hop-to like he should. I think he's broken. I'm going to get a different one.

BLACKIE: It's probably just a trace mineral deficiency.

JULIA: What's that supposed to mean?

BLACKIE: Chemicals, little lady, chemicals.

JULIA: What are you talking about?!

BLACKIE: He's probably just broken.

JULIA: Yeah.

(Enter EMILY *with black elephant.)*

JULIA: Not that one. I don't want Blackie to be the black one.

EMILY: I'm not going to get the other elephant. This one's fine.

JULIA: I don't want Blackie to be the black one.

EMILY: Nobody cares what you want, you mutated irrationally unkind person, you.

JULIA: Look who's calling who mutant, you crippled, freako, strange thing.

EMILY: I'm not strange.

JULIA: You are. You and your whole family. Why did Esther stop the suicide? Nobody ever stops once they've started. My female elder went stage one, two, three, four and then jumped off a bridge. Good riddance. And don't give me that story about how she was just looking for dirt. I'm not stupid.

BLACKIE: No one would ever say you're stupid, that's true. But there are behavioral aberrations—not as familiar to most people as the suicide—that resemble, but do not parallel the suicide. Esther's temporary obsession with dirt could be so classified.

JULIA: Esther? You call the woman Esther?

EMILY: *(Fast)* Yeah. She made him. She can't stand to be called "miss."

JULIA: "Miss" is a sign of respect. It's required. You made Blackie break rules! You're a whole family of unmanageable eliminatables. You've unsettled my calm! I'm going to report you. There's no reason to keep you. There's no reason to keep any of you. Gene's never going to help in the lab, and the whole house is just getting creepier and creepier. I'm going to complain. I'm gonna get permission to take you away. Today. Now. *(She exits, taking the elephants.)*

(A moment of silence)

EMILY: They won't take me. *(Pause)* Dad won't let them.

(Pause. She screams, BLACKIE puts his arms around her, she continues to scream.)

(Enter JUNE, visibly pregnant and ESTHER)

JUNE: Is she gone?

ESTHER: You children have the most amazing lungs.

(EMILY stops screaming, starts to pant.)

JUNE: *(To BLACKIE)* My love.

(They kiss.)

JUNE: Touch for luck?

(BLACKIE touches her stomach. ESTHER comes over and fits her knitting over JUNE's stomach.)

BLACKIE: We're going to need some luck. Please, Mom. Emily, calm down.

JUNE: It's a perfect fit, Mom.

BLACKIE: I need to think.

(EMILY starts upstairs.)

BLACKIE: Emily, come back. We're going to work this out.

(Enter GENE.)

GENE: They took my boat!

ESTHER: Did you go out, Gene?

GENE: It's not in the slip. They took my boat!

BLACKIE: I took your boat.

ESTHER: You didn't tell me goodbye I love you, Gene.

GENE: You what?

BLACKIE: It's gone. Forever. Sunk, by now, I should think.

JUNE: Why?

BLACKIE: I needed to get your attention.

GENE: You have my undivided attention.

BLACKIE: Gene, Morris says all the black men in the city are off stoppers. The network is complete. We're going to capture the fleet.

GENE: Capture from who? Nobody goes on the ships anymore.

BLACKIE: That's the point. Morris thinks it'll be weeks before they figure out where we've all gone. We need your knowledge.

ESTHER: Which Morris is that?

BLACKIE: Morris, Julia's Morris.

ESTHER: You guys gotta come up with some different names.

BLACKIE: Gene, are you in or not?

GENE: You took my boat!

BLACKIE: I'm offering you a fleet!

(EMILY *screams.*)

GENE: Hey, hey. What?

EMILY: You and your puffy bellies and pitiful schemes! You don't even care that I'm slotted for elimination this afternoon!

GENE: What?!

JUNE: Oh, no!

BLACKIE: We unsettled Julia's calm.

(*Everyone is silent.*)

BLACKIE: She'll be back soon with the sack. That's why we have to act now.

JUNE: I'm going to be sick.

EMILY: Big deal. I'm going to be dead.

GENE: Take...Emily? Really...take her?

BLACKIE: Yes, Gene. Take her. Really.

GENE: What...

BLACKIE: I'm trying to think.

GENE: I'll tell them I'll code for them. I *will* code for them. I'll do anything they want. They can't take Emily.

ESTHER: Gene, you can't, you mustn't, it's too awful.

BLACKIE: No, Gene. We'll find another way.

GENE: Oh, yeah, big shot. It's all right for me to code for you. I just can't code to save my daughter's life.

BLACKIE: Code for me? What are you talking about?

GENE: You want me to code a new race of black people. I know that.

BLACKIE: Who told you that?

GENE: I figured it out.

BLACKIE: No, Gene, no more scientific fast fix.

JUNE: Oh, Dad. We've already started a new race of black people.

BLACKIE: Black*ish* people.

GENE: Then why's it so all fired important for me to go along on this expedition?

BLACKIE: We don't want you to code. We want you to fish.

GENE: Fish?!

BLACKIE: We're counting on you to feed the entire fleet. You and Esther.

GENE: Yeah?

BLACKIE: And to teach every single Morris how to sing.

JULIA: (*Offstage. Banging on the door*) Open up. Open up in there! I know you're in there. Open the door.

ESTHER: Don't answer.

BLACKIE: Let *me* play this game.

(BLACKIE *opens the door.* JULIA *enters. She is carrying a black sack and a gag.*)

JULIA: The game's up. My complaint has been recognized and validated. We're taking Emily away. Help me pack her up, Blackie.

BLACKIE: Yes, Miss. What's the identifying mark?

JULIA: Her stupid gimp walk. What'd you think?

BLACKIE: That's a good idea. Give me the sack.

EMILY: *(Scared)* Morris?

JULIA: Of course it's a good idea.

JUNE: What are you doing?

ESTHER: You're not really going to take her away?

JULIA: Just shut up, all of you.

(In a swift and furious motion, BLACKIE throws the sack over JULIA's head.)

BLACKIE: Ahhhhh.

GENE: What should I do?

BLACKIE: The foot. Get Emily's foot.

(GENE grabs the foot from its place in the corner and puts it on JULIA. BLACKIE gags her through the sack and ties her up.)

GENE: Right.

(They put the foot on JULIA.)

BLACKIE: June, help everybody pack. Take medicine and any knowledge books we might be able to use. Gene, bring your rod.

GENE: Right.

BLACKIE: Esther, the vinegar.

ESTHER: I won't clean!

BLACKIE: It's a good antiseptic!

ESTHER: Then I'll bring it.

BLACKIE: Get Emily's elephants out of the stretch.

EMILY: What for?

BLACKIE: We will need them for our history lessons.

GENE: She's ready.

(JULIA *limps around in the sack.*)

GENE: What next? What next?!

BLACKIE: Morris and I will take her to the Eliminator. The initial identification is the limp. They won't know who it is until they take the sack off.

EMILY: What if they don't take the sack off?

GENE: Emily... Listen to Morris.

BLACKIE: We are delivering a package. That's all we're doing. What they do with the package belongs to their history, not to ours. I'll be back soon.

GENE: What do we do?

BLACKIE: Get ready to board ship.

GENE: Right. I can do that.

BLACKIE: Touch for luck?

(BLACKIE *touches* JUNE's *stomach and so does everyone else as the lights fade.*)

END OF PLAY

CPSIA information can be obtained
at www.ICGtesting.com
Printed in the USA
LVHW052320261118
598362LV00006B/180/P

9 780881 450750